Bullies Be Gone! Project™

Poetry Book

By Al Johnson

ISBN

Manufactured in the United States of America

Illustrations by Shanna Lim

Table of Contents

Introduction

In today's headlines, there have been incidents involving harassment of children and teens directly related to vicious, homophobic, cyberspace, racial, and other forms of bullying. The pain, anguish, and heartbreak of bullying victims can be overwhelming. Even supposedly mature politicians, religious leaders, and others are vociferous in a homophobic and vitriolic tone toward anyone with different lifestyles or points of view. Easily influenced children and teens hear these confusing tones of discord and may likely soon emulate in some unhealthy manner.

During his presidency, President Obama's Administration sent a "Dear Colleague" letter to schools across the country outlining their legal obligation to protect all students from harassment and bullying.

So-called anti-bullying experts give limited or non-comprehensive viable solutions to prevent or eliminate bullying. There is a vital need to empower children and teens with effective methods for solving a bullying problem with or without outside intervention. Through my Young, Alert, and Aware Program, now the Bullies Be Gone! Project, ages, 9–17, I have successfully taught bullying prevention as well as safety, awareness, racial harmony, and self-confidence to thousands of children, teens, and adults, in California since 1985.

Ultimately, the child or teen must solve their own bullying problem for it to be effectively and permanently eliminated through the process of self-empowerment. Possession of the necessary skills, knowledge, and confidence to do so is paramount. I have asked countless numbers of children: If they were or saw others being bullied, whether there was an adult present at that precise time. The answer has always been a resounding *NO!* The adult appears after the fact. The child could be harmed mentally and, possibly physically. If the bullying continues, which it will, without effective intervention, the harm the child/teen suffers will only become more severe, possibly lasting a lifetime.

My decision to write this book was for many reasons. I reflected to my childhood, teenage years, and as a young adult. I successfully learned how to prevent or eliminate bullying. I was raised in the inner cities of Jonesboro, AK and Kansas City, MO where, at the time, there was overt, mandated racial discrimination and segregation. Blacks were unfairly exposed to very similar forms of bullying that children suffer from today, i.e. derogatory name-calling, threats of physical harm, belittling, and other forms of debasement.

In addition, there was bullying within our segregated neighborhood. The internet did not exist, however, the negative effects of being bullied were quite personally devastating and impacting, as today.

At a very young age, I quickly learned effective methods of solving any bullying problem that arose. Gays, straight kids, and teens were empowered and street-smart, simply because they had to be to survive in that kind of climate. I have incorporated many of these strategies into my *Bullies Be Bone! Project's Comprehensive 8-Week Program* on bullying elimination and prevention. This poetic, fun, instructive, inspirational, motivational, and informative book, teaches children and adults effective methods of independently solving a bullying problem or potential one. "*Words are very powerful, they can harm, hurt, and even kill. Words are also very powerful when they build self-confidence, empower, and heal.*" The words in *Bullies Be Gone! Project* are designed to do the latter and *Self-Empower* children, teens, and adults.

Important messages to bullies to cease their inappropriate behavior are also vital components of the Bullies Be Gone! Project. **A Parent/Teacher's Manual & Student Training Manual accompanies this book outlining in detail methods of how to apply these *vital life skills* with children and teens.** *Bullies Be Gone! Project should be required supplemental education in secondary schools.* My book includes many of the language arts, reading, and English standards students are required to learn. In addition, *social skills* and *racial harmony, understanding, and tolerance,* which are not taught to any moderate extent in most schools, are taught in the Bullies Be Gone! Project.

The reader will find in each instructional and transformable poem *words, phrases,* and *stanzas* in **bold print**. These are highlighted as key elements of each poem for vocabulary building, critical thinking, critical discussion, creativity, and impacting messages of each poem. The teacher and parent should use these key areas to enhance the learning process for children and teens. (See parent/teacher training manual) In addition, each *illustration* accompanying a poem has a *hidden theme, as well as the theme of the poem itself,* which should be clearly understood by the child and teen.

The main objective of the Bullies Be Gone! Project is to empower children and teens to eliminate or prevent a bullying problem, with or without adult or peer intervention via Poetic Self-Empowerment and much more! Enjoy!

Acknowledgements

I would like to thank all those that have played a vital role in the writing of this book. From my early childhood years, many people whom I have long since been out of contact with, played a vital role in the content. Those experiences inspired many of the poems. More than two decades of teaching *Special Education* at the secondary level, and firsthand interactions with students of all ethnic backgrounds have been an inspiration for many of the poems in the *Bullies Be Gone! Project*. I thank those of you who granted me the opportunity to listen and observe your joy, grief, and pain, as they related to your life's experiences with others different than you. You shared your experiences with either being bullied or being the bully. Your experiences are reflected in the poems and illustrations.

I would like to give special thanks to Damaris Rosado, who has been there for me in the good times and the not so good ones. She always gives me the will to pursue my goals and persevere. Her continuous support in all my creative endeavors is highly appreciated and I am fortunate to have her as part of my life.

Bullies Be Gone! Project is a book addressing the negative impact bullying has on our youth today and their future. Effective ways for children, teens, and young adults to prevent being bullied are outlined. Obvious powerful messages to bullies to cease their inappropriate behavior are also outlined in the poems.

I thank a greater power that has blessed me with the gift and opportunity to express my thoughts and passions. Peace, harmony, tolerance, and understanding regardless of size, gender, race, religion, sexual preference, or any other difference, are what humankind should seek to embrace. Enjoy!

I'm Bouncing Back

I'm Bouncing Back

Yes, I'm bouncing back from a state of sadness and **gloom**.

I can't allow this sad state of mind to **linger and loom**.

No one, especially a kid like me, should be made to feel this way.

I'm unhappy because I'm being bullied. I'm sad almost every day.

I've decided **I'm bouncing back** to my good old days when life was full of nothing but lots of fun.

So, those of you who've been bullying me on line and at school, I have an important news flash for you, I'm bouncing back. The days of you bullying me are over and done.

Even better, though it may not be easy at first, you might try real hard ending your bullying ways. Why not switch to a more harmonious track?

Because lots of kids I know who have been bullied, just like me, are quickly, going to start bouncing back.

Al Johnson

I'm So Much Better Than You

I'm So Much Better than You

I'm so much better than you.

I'm not bragging, just telling you the truth.

You see, I'm so much better than you because I don't bully other kids like you do.

I don't call kids nasty names, make them feel bad, or do mean things to them like you do.

That makes me so much better than you in almost every way.

Maybe you should start **looking up to kids like me, instead of kids like you**; you might soon experience brighter and happier days.

The **fleeting moments of power and popularity**, you falsely believe you have, soon will **vanish** to a place where they belong, to a **world of untruth**.

More and more bullied kids are going to stand up to bullies like you and loudly **proclaim**, "I'm so much better than you!"

Al Johnson

I'm Not Going To Be Afraid Anymore

I'm Not Going to Be Afraid Anymore

I'm not going to be afraid anymore of you and your bullying ways.

You've been bullying me over and over, day after miserable day.

You call me names, sometimes push and shove, say bad things to me, and spread rumors about me to other kids.

I told my parents, the teachers, and principal too. You always lie and say bullying is not something you do or ever did.

So, it's obvious to me that I must solve my own bullying problem by taking a stronger stand.

I'm not going to be afraid of you anymore, this I hope you clearly understand.

Short of having to fight you, unless you provoke me, you will no longer bully me.

Can you hear the strength, sincerity, and passion in my voice? I'm not going to be afraid of you anymore. It would be a very wise thing for you to immediately take **heed**.

Al Johnson

You're The Weak One

You're the Weak One

You're the weak one, you're a bully. The weak one is for sure, not me.

The bully is always the weak one, but your weakness, you can't seem to clearly see.

So, I'm going to try and **shed** a little light on your **weak and inappropriate** ways.

Your weakness began on your very first bullying day.

Your false sense of power is not strength at all; it's a cry for help desperately trying to break through.

Never thought I'd say this to a bully, but I feel a little sorry for you.

Weak bullies like you always seek to find other kids they can dominate.

Bullies do this with vicious words, distasteful actions, and misguided hate.

Is being a weak bully the **banner** you want to always carry, as the precious years of your life pass by?

Get rid of the bully banner forever; create one that shows respect, understanding, and tolerance for others, and always proudly hold your magnificent new banner very high.

Al Johnson

Hateful Words

Hateful Words

Do you have any idea how much hateful words hurt those kids you're **spewing** them out to?

If you are a bully who uses them, you need to know they hurt deeply and could scar a kid for life. Is that what you really want to do?

It may seem like innocent fun when you're bullying other kids. The truth is it's not!

If you're a bully, because of the **negative impact** you can have on another kid, you must immediately stop!

I once thought bullying was cool, too, so I would say hateful words to other kids just to see how they would react.

I would say hateful words to their face. I would say them behind their back.

Then, out of nowhere, I heard the same kind of hateful words, meant for me.

I didn't like it a bit; in fact, I was hurt and angry as can be.

So, I immediately stopped using hateful words. I'm so glad I did.

No one deserves to hear hateful words, especially coming from another kid.

Al Johnson

I'm So Much Stronger Than You

I'm So Much Stronger than You

I'm so much stronger than you.

I'm stronger because of the mean and disrespectful things you do.

You enjoy bullying me and other kids too. You don't even care if what you say and do makes a kid feel terrible or not.

The nasty words you say and things you do always used to hurt a lot.

You may be bigger than me in physical size.

But physical size is not where **true inner strength** lies.

Suddenly, I'm **convinced** I'm stronger than you, because to other kids I'm always **respectful and kind**.

My parents have taught me that real strength comes from what's in a person's heart and mind.

So, the next time you try bullying me, before you try, I have a powerful message for you.

I will no longer be the sad bullied kid left to hang my head in shame. I now truly believe I'm so much stronger than you.

You might try to test me once or twice with those mean and nasty things you say and do.

I'm here to tell you don't even try it, you'll be wasting your time. By chance if you **mistakenly** do, you'll quickly see in more ways than one,

I'm so much stronger than you!

Al Johnson

Look At How I Walk Now

Look at How I Walk Now!

Because I was being bullied over and over again, you could just look at me and immediately see something was wrong.

It was clear that I was not a happy kid. I certainly didn't feel very strong.

My shoulders sagged, my chin almost **anchored** on my chest.

I didn't smile, have fun with my friends, and laugh a lot like kids should do. My life was a mess.

I walked like I was a hundred years old, almost afraid to take the next step.

There was no energy in my stride, there was no pep.

Then one day I looked in the mirror and decided that enough is enough. No kid deserves feeling sad, angry, and depressed all the time.

Adults nor my peers couldn't really solve my bully problem. They could help, but the real solution was for me to find.

I suddenly realized I needed to learn to take control, stand up to the bully, no matter how scary it might be.

I needed to begin walking with a tremendous air of self-confidence. I needed to start looking strong and powerful for the world to see.

To do this, I had to find a new way to react to the bully, somehow.

So, I made me a sign with big letters. Every day, I read it over and over, held it high, parading throughout the house. My sign changed my body language. It made me feel stronger. My sign reads: LOOK AT HOW I WALK NOW!

Al Johnson

No Longer Will You Bully Me

No Longer Will You Bully Me

The days of you bullying me are over as of this precise moment in time.

Yes, I mean it! I will back up my words in any **peaceful way** if I have to, for you to get the message. **I will no longer be yanked from your bullying-victim-line**.

No longer will you bully me at school, in the neighborhood, or on the internet.

I have empowered myself with self-confidence and pride like never before. Weaknesses I had that you took advantage of are gone for good. Yep, my **mindset** has changed just like that.

No longer will you bully me.

If you try, an unpleasant surprise you will quickly see.

I told you when you first started bullying me, I didn't want any trouble. But you didn't stop. And I was first unable to muster up the self-confidence to make you quit, like I could.

Now if you continue to try to bully me, you'll see a side of me you've never seen before. I promise, for you, the outcome won't be very good.

I hope you take my words to heart, and end your bullying ways as fast as can be.

I can't speak for other kids you might be bullying, but no longer will you bully me.

Al Johnson

You Weren't Born A Bully

You Weren't Born a Bully

You weren't born a bully, what happened along the way?

Did you just, all of a sudden, declare that you were going to be one and get joy from making other kids fell lousy day after day?

Were you bullied yourself? So, to get back at other kids, you decided to be the big bad bully too?

You find kids that you can easily **intimidate** because you know they're not physically strong as you.

You weren't born a bully, you allowed yourself to become one because you wanted to.

You can just as easily change and become a nice kid, and not bully anyone anymore; it's really not that hard to do.

I'll gladly help, be your friend if you like. Maybe together we can find a way to end your bullying ways.

You weren't born a bully, you were born to be a nice and kind kid. Why not start today!

Al Johnson

I'm As Self-Confident As Can Be

I'm as Self-Confident as Can Be

For a while, I let the bully steal my self-confidence away from me. Maybe it was never there.

The bully caused me to hang my head and question my **inner strength**. Sometimes I just sat around doing nothing, with a blank stare.

Bullies have a way of making you feel much smaller and weaker than you really are.

However, kids, your self-confidence can destroy the bully by you discovering who you really are.

Bullies want to keep a kid weak, with a confused mind,

That way the bully can take advantage of a kid, time after time.

Lucky for me, I found my self-confidence. It was anxious to surface. I just hadn't found it yet, even though it was always there.

Powerful self-confidence is in all kids, that includes you. It sometimes gets lost along the way; kids need to just find out where.

Here's to your new self-confidence that you will soon find. With it, you will surely defeat the bully.

I once was a victim of the bully too, but not anymore. **I'm as self-confident as can be**.

Al Johnson

My Mental Toughness

My Mental Toughness

My mental toughness wasn't anywhere to be found when you started bullying me.

I didn't think much of myself; your bullying made me feel small and weak.

I spent a lot of time being angry and crying. I didn't laugh like before, not very much at all.

You were winning, and what little pride I had left was sinking fast. I felt like banging my head against the wall.

Then my parents told me that bullies might sometimes be physically strong, but mentally they're very weak.

They told me to develop my mental toughness, by doing so, the bully I could easily defeat.

So, I began thinking I was strong, in body and mind.

And you know what? The more I thought about being mentally tough, the more confidence I seemed to find.

Mental toughness is a powerful tool that all kids should develop, have, and use.

If bullies happen to enter your space, the bully will sense your mental toughness. Bullies will immediately know, trying to bully you, will result in a situation where he/she will surely lose.

Al Johnson

I Strongly Suggest You Stop Bullying

I Strongly Suggest You Stop Bullying

I want you to carefully listen to what I am saying. I strongly suggest you stop bullying me.

I can't speak for another kid you might be bullying, but I can surely speak for me.

I've had just about enough of your stupid bullying ways.

You will not bully me again, not another single day.

Yeah, you are bigger and more popular than I am, but that doesn't matter anymore. I've decided I have to stand up to you.

Teachers, principals, my parents, or any other adult cannot solve my bullying problem. I have to! Adults are not around when you do the stupid stuff you do.

I'll say it again and again, shout it out if necessary, "I strongly suggest you stop bullying me."

Wow! Just saying that makes me feel so much stronger. Suddenly, the nasty things you say and the stupid stuff you do mean nothing to me.

You'll be much better off finding someone else to bully, you're wasting your **meaningless time** coming around my door.

Hello and goodbye, you will not bully me anymore!

Al Johnson

No Adult Around

No Adult Around

There is no adult around when you bully me.

The adult comes after the bullying is over, your stupid bullying they never see.

Too many times the adult that was not around when you were bullying me,

When told about it, doesn't even take your bullying seriously.

Too many adults think that some bullying is a natural thing for kids growing up.

There's nothing natural about being called nasty names that hurt deeply, and being pushed and shoved.

Why is there no adult around when bullying happens, especially at school?

Having another kid bully you is never too cool.

Adults need to pay closer attention to bullying possibilities that are sometimes in plain view.

Sometimes adults that are supposed to be smart and protect kids, when it comes to bullying, don't seem to have a clue.

Adults should be more aware of what's going on with kids in the hallways, restrooms, on the internet, and on the school grounds.

Because it is never a good thing when a kid is bullied, and there is no adult around.

Al Johnson

I Will Not Be Your Victim Anymore

I Will Not Be Your Victim Anymore

I will not be your victim anymore, you've gone too far. I've had more than enough.

You've bullied me, made me cry, and made me sad and mad, too. You enjoy bullying and stuff.

Suddenly, when I woke up this morning, I decided I will not be your victim anymore.

I was surprised how strong I felt just saying those words to myself over and over as I walked out my front door.

"I will not be your victim anymore" are words that have a lot of power if kids who are being bullied truly believe.

If kids repeat, "I will not be your victim anymore," it could give a kid the determination to stop the bullying they need.

Those words sure gave me strength and confidence; they could do the same for you.

No kid deserves to ever be bullied. If you're a kid and you're being bullied, here's what I suggest you do:

Decide that you're no longer going to be bullied like before.

Say these words repeatedly to yourself, then say them to the bully with conviction, when you feel strong and confident: "I will not be your victim anymore!"

Al Johnson

Anti-Bullying Pill

Anti-Bullying Pill

Mom gives me a children's pill to help me get better when I have a cold.

Mom gives me vitamin pills, too. She says they will keep me from too soon growing old.

For kids, there seems to be a pill for almost everything.

But I've never heard of an anti-bullying pill for a kid, now that would be a very cool thing.

Kids could just take their anti-bullying pill before going to school.

Now that would be super cool.

The anti-bullying pill would make kids feel aware, confident, and strong.

The bully would know just by a kid's look of self-confidence, which kid took his/her anti-bullying pill that day. So, rather than hassle the kid, the bully would leave him/her alone.

I know there is no real anti-bullying pill. However, just maybe, kids could create one in their mind.

Kids could successfully create their anti-bullying pill as soon as they wake up and at their healthy breakfast time.

What kids think in their mind, will be how they react.

So, kids, before going to school, take your mind-created imaginary-anti-bullying pill. It could help you keep the bully far away and permanently off your back.

Al Johnson

Body Language

Body Language

Kids, your body language says a lot about you.

It tells the world if you have pride and confidence in almost everything you do.

If your shoulders are drooping and you appear to always be looking at the ground,

A bully will surely see your poor body language, and quickly decide you're the **perfect kid to hound**.

You must stand tall, walk with your chin up and shoulders back. You will be telling the world you're a kid that's alert and aware.

The bully will take one long look at you and conclude you're not a kid to be picked on. The best choice for the him/her will be to leave you alone and go elsewhere.

Be proud of who you are every day, display your pride from head to toe.

Your good body language will be a powerful tool for you to use. It may be all you need to prevent the bully from coming anywhere close.

Al Johnson

Parents Don't Bully Each Other

Parents Don't Bully Each Other

Kids learn from what their parents say and do.

If Mom and Dad are somehow bullying each other, kids will see, then guess what their kids might likely soon do.

Parents, please don't bully each other, doing so is a huge mistake.

You may not be aware, but you're probably training your children to respond to other kids the very same way.

Mom and Dad, if you are bullying each other and your kid gets in trouble for bullying at school, or on the internet too,

Mom and Dad, most of the blame could be placed squarely on you.

No one is insisting, as parents, how you should run your household.

However, by not bullying each other as adults, you increase the chances of your kids not becoming a bully ten-fold.

Parents, please don't bully each other. To not bully each other is a healthy thing for your kids and you.

No kid deserves to be bullied because they're different, small, overweight, or for any other reason. The same holds true Mom and Dad, for the person you're married to.

Al Johnson

Anti-Bullying Powder

Anti-Bullying Powder

I'm going to take my very effective anti-bullying powder with me to school.

If the bully gets in my space, I'll put my powder to good use.

Bullies aren't very smart, so I'm going to play with the bully's mind if he chooses to pick on me.

I'll pull my container of anti-bullying powder from my backpack and sprinkle it on the bully's knees.

The bully will be so confused his knees will **buckle,** and just like that, he will **crumble** to the ground.

The bully will be looking up at me, half my size, unable to stand, and looking like a clown.

In a firm voice, I'll tell the bully, "I only used a tiny bit of my magic powder and look what that did to you.

You're now the big bad bully who can't stand on his own two feet. I'll sprinkle more of my powder if necessary, then you'll really be in a soup."

Wow! Wouldn't it be nice if someone invented magic anti-bullying powder for a kid to use?

Then there would be no more worry about being bullied by any kid packing his anti-bullying powder at school.

Al Johnson

It's Never Too Late To Change

It's Never Too Late to Change

If you are a bully, you know you are, because it's what you've chosen to be.

You make excuses that you being a bully is someone else's fault. Unfortunately, the truth you refuse to see.

So you constantly search for easy victims. You want to destroy their confidence and self-esteem.

You don't care how other kids feel when you bully them. Because of your bullying, kids have nightmares instead of pleasant dreams.

I'm a kid just like you.

But I don't bully other kids, which I would never do.

Nowhere does it say you must be a bully for the rest of your life.

There is a good side of you that lies deep within. It's now asleep in the dark of night.

The good person you can be eagerly wants to spread its wings, bringing happiness, fun, joy, and eliminating shame.

Please remember, no matter how much you have bullied other kids, for a much happier life for you, it's never too late to change.

Al Johnson

Rumors Online

Rumors on Line

The rumors on line about me, coming from you, are lies and you know it.

Are you spreading rumors because you're jealous of me, and this is how you've chosen to show it?

Come on, is spreading vicious, stupid rumors the best you can do?

You are trying to destroy me, but the truth is, eventually, your lies are going to destroy you.

If your **intent** was to make me feel bad about myself, with rumors spreading all over the internet,

Congratulations, you **initially succeeded,** but I refuse to go into a shell-of-shame because of you. **I now declare your rumors meaningless at best**.

My parents and others that care about me have helped me find **my inner strength that was mired in quicksand**.

I looked in the mirror one day and decided no one can destroy me unless I allow him or her to. Moreover, I should be quite proud of who I am.

So, I strongly suggest you cease spreading your rumors and lies about me or anyone else throughout cyberspace.

Your tasteless rumors on line have no clout any more. I declare them **baseless** and empty threats. In the real world of decent, good, and respectful people where I live, your rumors have no place.

Al Johnson

Not Physically Fit Yet

Not Physically Fit Yet

True, I 'm not physically fit as I would like or need to be.

But because I'm not, that doesn't give you the right to bully me.

If you were in my place, you wouldn't like to hear the things you say and do to me.

I'm telling you to stop now with your bullying; I'm as fed up with it as can be.

Yes, to your surprise, I'm standing up to you. You will not bully me anymore.

I don't care how tough you think you are. I'm no longer afraid of you. Fear has taken a permanent hike, with a strong wind behind it, out my door.

.Bullies like you really have very little self-confidence. You're a very weak person inside and out.

Bullies look for an easy victim, someone they can **control and dominate**. That's why you chose me and for a while I gave you that needed **clout**.

As of today, your false power is a big zero when it comes to me. As far as I'm concerned, you're just all wet.

Thank you! You have given me the **inspiration** to shape up and be quite proud of who I am, even though I'm not physically fit yet.

Al Johnson

Who Bullied You?

Who Bullied You?

Who bullied you? What did it feel like being bullied by someone?

Did they call you nasty names and push you around? Did they destroy your will to have fun?

Who bullied you? Did they threaten you, leaving you full of fear?

Did the bully leave you all lonely and confused, causing so many things in your life to seem unclear?

Who bullied you? Who caused you to sometimes be afraid to go to school?

I know **the bullying you suffered** didn't make you feel very cool?

For **clarity,** I just thought I'd ask who bullied you?

Many kids who bully other kids, were once bullied, too.

If none of those nasty things happened when you were being bullied, you surely wouldn't know how I feel.

You wouldn't understand or care when you bully me, if I lose my pride and self-confidence. My fun and laughter, is what you want to steal.

But I'm sure you do know how I feel because when you were being bullied, you felt the same lousy way, too.

I hope you get this message; you don't have to and shouldn't bully me or anyone else because of who bullied you!

Al Johnson

One Time

One Time

If you bully another kid just one time, that's one time too many.

The pain a kid suffers from your one-time bullying could cause a kid to mentally lose his/her identity.

One time is always too many for anything that is wrong.

You need to know that being a bully really doesn't somehow make you very strong.

There was one time I thought about being a bully, too, just like you.

But it took me only one time to think about it and conclude bullying wasn't a nice or smart thing for me to do.

I suggest you take just one time to sit and think deeply about the nasty things you're doing to other kids, you might be surprised.

One time of careful and heartfelt deep thinking could clear your mind and open your eyes.

Hopefully, you will take one time to think differently about being a bully and plainly see,

There is never a good reason to be a bully, but there are always wonderful reasons to be the best person that you can be.

Al Johnson

You Tried To Defeat Me

You Tried to Defeat Me

You tried to defeat me with the **foul words** you say constantly.

To your surprise, instead of your words tearing me down, they lifted me up so I could clearly see.

You're just a lonely bully without any real true friends.

Kids that do hang around with you are just as **pathetic**, too. I suggest you all find a way for your bullying to end.

You tried to defeat me and probably other kids, too.

For a while, you were successful because I was afraid of you.

But my parents and others told me to be confident and strong, no matter how hard it was for me.

They told me this over and over. One day I was suddenly convinced **bullies prey on weak kids to succeed**.

I don't feel weak anymore. In fact, I'm feeling very strong.

You tried to defeat me, it didn't work. News flash! From this point on, you'd better leave me alone!

Al Johnson

Somewhere Inside You

Somewhere inside You

Do you really enjoy being a bully, always acting tough?

You go around with a frown on your face saying **filthy words** to kids. You know what! We kids are tired of hearing that stuff.

Somewhere inside you, there's a nice kid just waiting for a chance to shine.

Somewhere inside you, there's **peace and harmony eager to surface**. Don't you think now would be the perfect time?

Somewhere inside you, there's an **abundance** of joy and cheer.

If you will allow all these wonderful things somewhere inside you to surface, you'll no longer spread confusion, hate, and fear.

Your bullying days will be over forever, you'll have lots of great friends, many of them brand new.

Please let the good and kind person you can be, **reveal** itself for everyone to clearly see. A nice and kind kid is eagerly awaiting somewhere inside you.

Al Johnson

What Path In Life Are You On?

What Path in Life Are You On?

What path in life are you on?

If you are a kid that bullies other kids, your current path is unfortunately wrong.

If you bully another kid face to face or on the internet,

The path you've chosen to take so far is one you should quickly cease to take and soon forget.

What path are you on, where will your path lead?

Will your path take you to a life of respect and happiness, or one of fear and hate? Which path will you heed?

Even as a kid, you have control over the choices you make.

What path in life are you on? What path will you **consistently** take?

Please take the path of treating every kid, no matter their size, gender, sexual preference, or race, as you would want to be. It simply boils down to showing respect for others in a civil tone.

Look in the mirror, look in your eyes, the kid staring back at you will reveal what path in life you're on.

Al Johnson

Face To Face

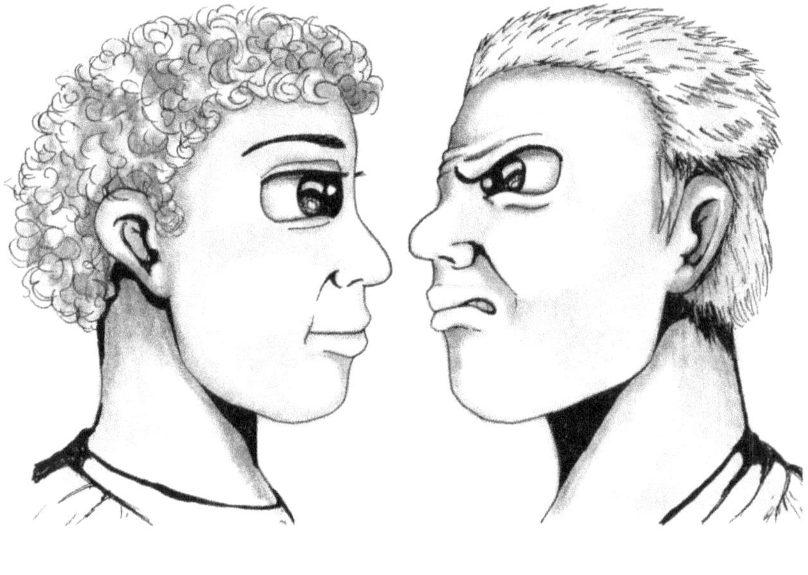

Face to Face

Let's you and I meet face to face.

This time you will not bully me because I'm going to put you in your rightful place.

Yes, it's me, the kid you've been bullying, calling for a face to face solution.

So far, every time you get in my face, you've **intimidated** me. I'm always left feeling weak and small, in a world of confusion.

When you see me face to face this time, you'll see a different me, as you've never seen before.

Confidence will be written all over my face. I'll look you straight in the eyes and tell you in a firm voice that you will not bully me anymore.

No, I'm not asking you to meet me face to face to do physical battle. But I will battle you with my mind.

You will absolutely know that you have bullied me for the very last time.

In case you don't want to meet me face to face, not knowing what to expect, you may feel it won't be time for you well spent.

Just maybe we can meet face to face soon, not as enemies, but as respectful friends.

Al Johnson

Wear A Smile On Your Face

Wear a Smile on Your Face

Try wearing a smile on your face instead of that ugly, bullying frown.

If you try wearing a smile on your face, you'll be a much happier kid than you are now.

Even though you might get pleasure from bullying other kids, you're not smart enough to know deep inside you're quite sad.

Deep inside, you truly know the bullying you're doing is bad.

If you'll learn to wear a smile on your face, the anger that burdens you will soon go away.

It will be impossible for you to bully another kid when you're truly smiling every day.

Your smiles will destroy the anger inside you and, very soon, permanently, your bullying will disappear for good.

Then you'll be known as the nice and friendly kid that you really can be, at school, on line, and in your neighborhood.

Al Johnson

Smile On My Face

Smile on My Face

Finally, I have a smile on my face; it's been missing for a long time.

My smile disappeared when the bully kept picking on me all the time.

Now that I look back, it was easy for the bully to take the natural smile on my face away from me.

I made the mistake of allowing the bully from the very beginning to be the one in control. This fact, I was too blind to see.

It's hard to smile when the nasty names the bully calls you keep ringing in your ears and mind.

The smile on my face I always used to wear was taken over by sadness, anger, and gloom. I felt miserable all the time.

The bully was the one wearing a phony smile. I really didn't know what to do.

One day, I actually got help from another kid, a friend of mine who had been bullied, too.

He told me bullies always expect a kid they are bullying to never stand up to them and put a bully in his/her place.

My friend told me his first step in defeating the bully and regaining his confidence, was to get rid of sadness caused by the bully. He did this by wearing an everyday smile on his face.

Al Johnson

Seven Days A Week

Seven Days a Week

Not for one day, two, or three, but for seven days a week, you'll no longer bully me.

It took some time for me to clearly see, to defeat you, exactly how I really needed to be.

I've decided that for seven days a week, I will be confident and strong.

Bullies like you will then get the message to leave me alone.

I never look for trouble as you do, l enjoy being nice and having good and kind friends.

You enjoy making other kids afraid to come to school because they know what bullies **intend**.

I'm going to share my seven days a week pledge with other kids you might seek out to bully.

Then everywhere you look, there will be nothing but confident kids all around you. I know that's not what you really want to see.

If you stop your bullying ways, you know how your life could be,

Full of fun, true friends, and shared laughter, seven days a week.

Al Johnson

Do Bullies Ever Cry?

Do Bullies Ever Cry?

Do bullies ever cry? You know what? I believe they do.

Bullies always put on a tough and strong front, which is designed to scare and confuse you.

My parents told me if you get a bully to spill his/her real emotions; you would be shocked at what you would hear and see.

Bullies are really hurting inside. They hide it by bullying kids like you and me.

Do bullies ever cry? It very much seems like they do.

Then bullies must need help in facing the truth.

How can kids being bullied help a bully? What can kids do?

If you're one of those kids, you can decide to stand up to the bully and not let him/her bully you.

You can tell the bully what he/she is doing is not right.

You can do this in a calm but firm way that doesn't cause a fight.

Make sure while you do, look the bully straight in the eyes.

You can do this with confidence because you know what; the bully doesn't know you know, that bullies do cry.

Al Johnson

You Hide In Front Of A Computer

You Hide in Front of a Computer

You're a bully that hides in front of a computer sending out messages of lies, disrespect, and hate.

If you have to hide in front of a computer to bully me, you're not the least bit brave at all. In fact, you're a phony and a fake.

I actually feel sorry for you as you **hopelessly linger** in your **pathetic state**.

The truth about me or any kid you're bullying will eventually come out. Truth is frightening for you, isn't it? Because **the truth will seal your fate**.

You hide in front of a computer for hours at a time.

Your time would be better spent if you somehow discovered ways, with other kids, you could become nice and kind.

You hide in front of a computer going about your daily sour routine of bullying other kids.

One day your computer will crash and along with it, your despicable bullying empire, too. Just maybe then, you'll feel somewhat sorry for all the unnecessary bullying you did.

Al Johnson

Do The Unexpected

Do the Unexpected

Bullies are used to their victims acting in a particular way.

Therefore, a bully can easily take advantage of a kid that reacts the same way, day after day.

If kids learn to do the unexpected when a bully gets in their space,

It could create confusion in the bully's mind and put him/her in an unwanted and uncomfortable place.

The bully expects kids to be afraid of them all the time.

Kids, do the unexpected, though it may be hard at first. Show no visible fear. Show confidence just by your powerful body language and the look in your eyes.

Bullies usually speak to their victims in a commanding voice.

Do the unexpected, your voice can be just as commanding, if not more so. Be serious about what you say to the bully. It's your best choice.

A bully may put his/her unwanted hands on you.

Do the unexpected, the bully's **uninvited hands** must be quickly removed.

You can ask the bully to remove his/her hands in your commanding voice.

If he/she doesn't, you must physically take them away, then leave the scene quickly. **Fighting the bully should never be your first choice**.

To do the unexpected could be anything done out of the ordinary, using your look, voice, body, or mind.

By doing the unexpected, a kid could eliminate or prevent a bullying problem for the very last time.

Al Johnson

Anti-Bully Juice

Anti-Bully Juice

For breakfast this morning, I had eggs, milk, orange juice, and my special anti-bully juice, too.

I had my tasty, heaping glass of anti-bully juice; it's so good for my body and mind. It always makes me feel very strong. After drinking it, I look forward to going to school.

Kids, if you haven't been drinking your anti-bully juice each and every day, now is a great time to start.

After drinking your anti-bully juice, any kid who wants to bully you will find their success in doing so quite hard.

Your anti-bully juice will give you an **invisible protective shield** the bully cannot **penetrate** nor see.

I bet anti-bully juice will work for you, too. It has always worked for me.

You might be thinking you can't wait to get some. **Where do Mom and Dad buy you anti-bully juice?**

They don't have to buy it. It's already in your home. And if they do have to buy it, it's inexpensive. All you have to do now is put it to good use.

Grab an empty glass, fill it with water from a bottle or the tap. Take a deep breath; let it out slowly before you drink, clear your mind, and make a powerful promise to yourself, one, that no matter what, you must do.

Promise yourself and really mean it, you'll never be bullied again! If you have to each day, reinforce that promise by drinking a healthy glass of your inexpensive and in great supply, anti-bully juice!

Al Johnson

Think On Your Feet

Think on Your Feet

When a bully gets in another kid's face, the bully's objective is to take control and instill fear.

The kid being bullied becomes confused, and often, their thinking becomes unclear.

Now the bully has the upper hand. The bully is totally in charge.

The kid being bullied must quickly think on his/her feet. If they have been trained to do so, this will not be very hard.

To think on your feet simply means deciding to get yourself out of a bully situation as quickly and safely as you can.

Here are some choices you have: Talk your way out of the bully situation, make any excuse necessary to leave the scene, use your strong convincing voice. The last resort is to aggressively use your hands.

Most kids who are bullied have no clue what it means to think on their feet.

Now you have an idea, but you'll need to learn more and then practice to make your training complete.

By having the ability to think on your feet, your chances of being caught off guard by a bully will be a lot less.

By having the ability to think on your feet in a bully situation, you could leave the bully confused. Hopefully, the bully quickly concludes, leaving you alone is probably the wisest thing to do next.

Al Johnson

My Difference Is My Strength

My Difference Is My Strength

The difference in the way I look, walk, talk, or what I prefer in life is not my weakness. Because of your misguided and intolerant beliefs, you need to know, my difference is my strength.

I'm not ashamed of who I am. No matter how many nasty things you say about me, my head will be held very high. **My difference is my strength**.

Unfortunately, you've chosen to live with your ignorance and hate. Unless you change, you'll carry that heavy burden for the rest of your miserable life.

That heavy load will eventually wear you down. You'll be stuck in quicksand, slowly sinking, as time rapidly passes you by.

You'll never be the good and kindhearted person you could have been. You'll never experience the brilliance of humankind.

My difference is my strength. I'm happy with and proud of who I am. My strength lies in my heart and mind.

Your **needless criticism** of me and others too, for **no viable reason**, shows how **shallow** a person you really are.

My difference is my strength. Do you even have the slightest clue that **your nasty tone unnecessarily, goes way too far?**

My difference is my strength. Your weakness lies in the disrespectful things you say and do.

My difference is my strength. However, you're not a lost cause. I truly believe there's still a **sliver of hope** for positive change, **longing** to come out, somewhere deep inside you!

If somehow, you haven't clearly understood this powerful message to you I've sent.

Emphatically, I say to you again, my difference is my strength!

MY DIFFERENCE IS MY STRENGTH!!

Al Johnson

You Don't Exist

You Don't Exist

I'm just a kid like you. But in my mind, if you're a bully, guess what! You don't exist, **you're just meaningless hot air**.

I learned that bullies like a lot of attention. They like a lot of **flare**.

Bullies usually get what they want by using a commanding voice, having a frown on their face, and a very unpleasant stare.

Well, since you don't exist in my mind, it's impossible for me to give you any attention or the least bit of concern or **fanfare**.

If you're a kid with a bullying problem, the next time a bully gets in your face, tell him/her they don't exist, they're nothing but hot air.

The bully will be confused and won't like what you say.

Leave the bully in his/her state of confusion by quickly and **cautiously** walking away.

The bully may or may not **pursue** you.

Don't be surprised by anything a bully might do.

Chances are the bully just may leave you alone.

If he/she doesn't, immediately tell the bully again, "they don't exist," this time do so in a very **convincing and commanding tone**.

Al Johnson

Justice Will Be Served

Justice Will Be Served

If you're a bully that constantly picks fights, spreads rumors, tell lies, and do **immature stupid stuff bullies do,** soon you'll be thrown a curve.

I'm here to tell you, if you're a bully, one day on you, justice will be served.

Hopefully, your justice will not be in a court of law. That could only mean you've been bullying way too many years, and your bullying has become quite severe.

The perfect time to stop your bullying is now, in your early years.

The justice that will be served if you continue to bully may be by another kid, one stronger, tougher, and not the least bit afraid of you.

If you try to bully this kid, the justice this kid will serve on you will be **very unpleasant**, that's nothing but the truth.

You have no idea who this powerful kid is. You don't know his/her size, gender, race, religion, or anything else. You don't have a clue.

If you make the mistake of bullying this kid, to your unwanted surprise, justice will be served on you so fast, for the rest of your life, bullying will be the last thing you'll ever want to do.

So, here is my strong suggestion to you: stop your bullying now! If you try hard, you really can **muster up** the necessary nerve.

If you don't very, very soon, on you I promise, justice will be served.

Al Johnson

Mental Weakness

Mental Weakness

If you're a bully, you have allowed mental weakness to control you instead of your potential mental strength.

You have a great mind like any other kid, but the very second you decided to bully another kid, you instantly became **mentally weak and dense**.

What makes you mentally weak is that you're totally unaware that you are.

If you were mentally strong, you'd know that bullying another kid is wrong. Unfortunately, you haven't come to that correct conclusion so far.

So, you continue to bully kids. Your mental weakness has the upper hand because you allow it to.

Are you so shallow and mentally weak that you're not fully aware that you have complete control over what you say and do?

Mental weakness can be **reversed**, almost in the time it takes to blink an eye.

At this very moment, if you mentally say to yourself you'll never bully another kid again, and you mean it, your mental weakness will never again **hover** over you, or even chance flying by.

Al Johnson

Your Mental Weakness

Your Mental Weakness

When you made the unwise decision to become a bully, your mental weakness took center stage.

The spotlight of stupidity shone brightly on you, revealing your mental weakness in all kinds of inappropriate ways.

You call kids **inappropriate** names, just to make them feel bad.

That's mental weakness I bet you never knew you had.

You spread rumors about kids around school and on the internet.

That's your mental weakness working overtime and, sadly, you don't even recognize it's a crippling weakness yet.

You hassle other kids because they're different than you.

Oops! There goes your mental weakness again, unable to see the tons of more positive things you could very easily do.

You enjoy intimidating kids smaller, making them scared and confused.

That's your mental weakness, totally out of control. You have allowed your mental weakness to get the better of you.

Your mental weakness will eventually wear you down. It'll be a gigantic unbearable heavy load, too heavy for you to carry around.

Why not lighten your load, stop your bullying now? You'll then smile more and lose forever that unbecoming bully frown.

Al Johnson

Isolated And Alone

Isolated and Alone

If you are a bully, you're isolated and alone.

There may be kids around you, but the nice kids don't stay very long. No one really likes a bully's nasty tone.

You would probably say you have plenty of great friends at school, in the neighborhood, and you're always talking to people on your cell phone.

I'm here to tell you, if you're a bully, although you're not intelligent enough to know it, you're really isolated and alone.

Those kids that do consider themselves your friends and hang out with you are mistakenly and unfortunately exactly like you.

The whole **disrespectful herd** of you **incompetent bullies** is isolated and alone, too.

The sad thing is, when you need a real helping hand, and someday you will, your so-called friends will be nowhere around. They will be long gone.

My parents have told me it is no fun, in fact it can be **devastatingly depressing**, as you grow older, to find yourself isolated and alone.

Al Johnson

Your Nasty Words Cannot Hurt Me

Your Nasty Words Cannot Hurt Me

You hoped the nasty words you said to me would hurt me so much that like a turtle, I would go into a **permanent shell**.

My parents told me not to give a bully that kind of satisfaction. From all the nasty words you said, guess what, I'm not feeling bad at all. In fact, I'm doing quite well.

Yes, your nasty words hurt me at first, just as you wanted them to.

I'm lucky to have parents, responsible adults, and even other kids, who showed me how to effectively handle bullies like you.

I don't care the least bit what you do anymore. I really don't care what you say.

Your nasty words cannot hurt me again. You tried putting me down, but with **self-determination** and help from others, I've been lifted up in every way.

I see you as a **small-minded bully,** with no positive direction.

I also see you as a kid who could be nice and kind to others, if you decide to **change your intentions**.

Just in case you refuse to change and continue with your bullying ways, declaring that's just how it's going to be,

I'm going to do all I can to spread my anti-bullying words to as many kids as I can. Then the next kid you try to bully, hopefully, will confidently say to you, "Your nasty words cannot hurt me."

Al Johnson

I Can See Right Through You

I Can See Right through You

I can see right through you. Bullies are as **transparent** as can be.

You act tough and strong, but what I see **reveals** you're weak.

You try to hide your weakness in every way you can by doing the nasty and dumb things you do.

Sorry, **concealment** is not working with me, I can see right through you.

If a kid is afraid of a bully, he/she can't possibly see how weak bullies really are.

Kids must be trained to clearly understand a bully is an open book that exposes **inner scars**.

To be able to see right through the bully is a special talent that all good kids must **possess**.

Each time a bully tries to **intimidate** another kid with the **intent** of making him/her feel bad and weak, it's always a test.

If the kid that's being picked on already knows this about a bully, and knows what to do,

The bully can be defeated, because the kid knows what the bully doesn't. The kid can tell the bully, "You will not bully me ever, I can see right through you!"

Al Johnson

Hear How I Talk Now

Hear How I Talk Now

Each time I was bullied, I began talking with no confidence, in a very soft and **ineffective** voice.

Your bullying made me feel like I had no other choice.

Your voice was strong it overpowered mine.

My voice became **very faint** when you were around. You made me feel weak and helpless all the time.

Your words **roared like thunder,** almost making me shutter and shake.

You made my words weak and meaningless because of the nasty things you'd say.

Each time you roared at me in your strong bully voice, I became more and more silent and fearful of you.

Every time you came into my space, **I was practically mute**.

The helpless feeling you caused somehow made me search for **inner strength I never knew I had**.

I discovered things inside of me, not known before, strengths I never knew I had.

I found an **inner voice, vibrant and strong,** just begging to come out.

The next time you try to bully me, my inner voice will cause your eardrums to explode with these words: "Hear how I talk now!"

Al Johnson

The Nerdy Looking Kid

The Nerdy Looking Kid

You started bullying me and I started feeling bad.

You took my confidence away, confidence I didn't know I had.

The more you bullied me, the worse I felt.

My mistake in the beginning was I didn't say anything or ask my parents or teachers for help.

Your bullying went on and on, day after lousy day.

You had power over me and I didn't know how to take it away.

One day this nerdy looking kid came up to me at school, looking like she just stepped out of a science book.

This kid was thin, wore thick glasses, but had a real confident look.

This kid told me she knew what I was going through with the bully. The same kid used to bully her, too.

I was more than shocked. I asked, "If she doesn't bully you anymore, how did you make it stop? What did you do?"

The nerdy looking kid told me this, as she looked straight in my eyes,

"I stopped thinking like a victim, walking like a victim; talking like a victim; looking like a victim; and being a victim. My confidence grew and grew as days passed by."

"The bully wasn't sure what was going on. I was showing my newly-found-confident attitude, the bully had never seen from me."

"She didn't like what she saw. I was doing stuff the bully didn't expect to see."

"I was showing her things that no kid she ever bullied had shown before."

"Very quickly, I saw the bully as having no power, and she knew I wasn't afraid, worried, or concerned with what she said or did, anymore."

"The bully very quickly stopped bothering me. She went searching for a new victim, and found you."

"If a nerdy looking kid like me can get rid of a bully problem by making some very important **self-empowering confident changes**, guess what? So can you, too!"

Al Johnson

You Must Solve Your Bullying Problem

You Must Solve Your Bully Problem

As a kid, you must eventually solve your bullying problem for it to permanently go away.

If you're being bullied, you must tell your parents, teachers, or any responsible adults. However, the bullying may continue the very same way.

You might be thinking, if adults can't solve my bully problem, who can?

The chances are no adult is around when you're being bullied. You're on an island with just you and the bully. You must learn to take a strong stand.

It may not be an easy task to solve your bully problem alone, but if you're taught how, it can and will be done.

The bully will see a stronger and more confident you and wonder where your new **self-empowering attitude** came from.

You must solve your bully problem and you can do it. There are certain skills you need to be shown.

These special skills you must learn and **hone**.

You'll maintain these skills for the rest of your life.

Then, no matter what age you are, when bullies sense and see your special skills, he/she will leave you alone and rapidly take flight.

Al Johnson

Being Street-Smart

Being Street-Smart

You may be asking yourself, "What does being street-smart mean and what does that have to do with me?"

Almost all kids are sheltered and protected by their parents or other responsible adults, in early childhood, that's how it should be.

When a bully hassles another kid, that kid is no longer under the **protective umbrella** of parents or responsible adults. The kid is left to **fend** for himself/herself, all too often, eventually in the mean streets.

If a kid is not street-smart, and most are not, the bully has the advantage. The bully is then tough to defeat.

Being street-smart is being confident, alert, aware, and having the ability to create confusion and doubt in the bully's mind.

This is not easy to do when a kid has been **sheltered** all the time.

Being street-smart is knowing words to say, when and how to say them, and specific actions to take, when a bully has decided he/she wants to bully you.

Being street-smart is knowing how to do exactly what a bully doesn't expect you to do.

Bullies carefully avoid street-smart kids, so make sure the bully quickly knows to stay away from you.

Street-smart kids **create on the fly**, as quick as can be.

A street-smart kid's **antennae** are sharply tuned for any negative possibility.

Street-smart kids quickly reverse the situation in their favor. Yes, a kid must be trained to be street-smart by someone who knows and understands the streets.

It may or may not be the parents who do the training; however, what a kid wants to avoid is for the street-smart training to come from the bully.

Al Johnson

Hitting "The Light Switch"

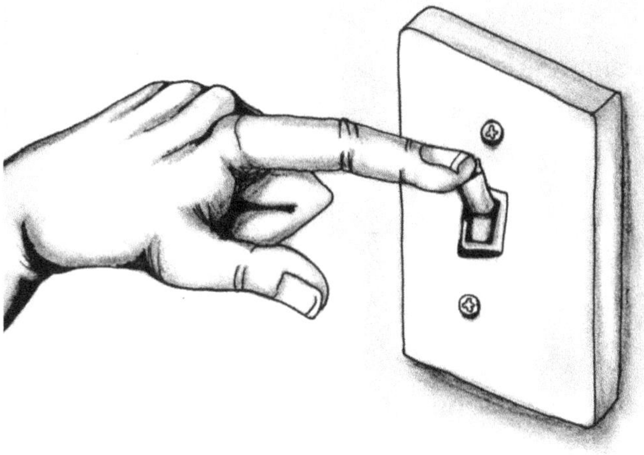

Hitting "the Light Switch"

In this poem, kids, you will learn how hitting "the light switch" could help you in a big way get rid of a bully.

Kids, "the light switch" is in your mind, a place where a bully cannot see.

You should only practice this drill at home, which is the correct thing to do.

Get your parents involved, so they can learn with you.

Go over to the light switch in your house; place your index finger on it so you can control it by flicking it back and forth or up and down.

Now, look directly at the lights you are about to make go on and off, those lights in the ceiling or at eye level. While hitting the light switch, concentrate on the lights, don't look all around.

Keep your eyes glued to the lights as you or your parents begin flicking them on and off. Do this very quickly about five or six times.

My question to you is, "How long did it take for the lights to go on and off?" Remember, hitting "the light switch" is all about your mind.

Did the lights go on and off in a matter of seconds, is that what you would say?

You would be correct if you said in no more than a second or two. You would be correct in every way.

As a kid, you might be asking what does this have to do with a bully? How does this help me?

Well, I will explain further, soon you will see.

If a bully ever comes around wanting to hassle you, it is **imperative** you immediately hit "the light switch" in your mind.

You must do it, when necessary, every single time.

Just as quickly as you saw the lights go on and off, it is **critical** you do the following three things with ease:

Relax, React, Respond as fast as the lights went on and off. The complete necessity of this drill you will soon see.

You will be taught the **Three R's** and how to apply them in the next poem, so you can perform under a bully's pressure, and **hopefully, perform without a glitch**.

What I want kids to learn from this poem and the one that follows is if a bully ever threatens, they must immediately know how to effectively hit "the light switch."

Al Johnson

Relax, React, Respond

Relax, React, Respond

Okay kids, in the poem before this one you learned about hitting "the light switch" in your mind to help you defeat the bully, if you ever have to.

I introduced the Three R's. Now you're going to learn what they mean and how to put them to good use.

Relax is the first thing you must do if the bully gets in your face. "So, how do I relax," you might say?

Take a quick, quiet, deep breath, inhale and draw the air in through your nose, exhale, quietly blow the air out through your mouth. Do this two or three times.

Imagine you are pinching a balloon that you just blew air into between your thumb and index finger to keep the air inside.

As soon as you take your finger and thumb away, the air rushes out, the balloon goes limp and becomes very relaxed.

By relaxing quickly in a bad situation, especially with a bully, your muscles don't become tense and your mind remains clear, now you can better ***React***.

React is to immediately decide how you're going to allow yourself to feel about this unwanted bully situation. **Proper relaxation should help you take control**.

You'll either feel scared, excited, very aware or unaware of your surroundings, confident or not, and ready, or not **ready to immediately take control**.

You will react in pretty much one of these ways.

Now you must decide how you're going to ***Respond***. Your goal is to cause the bully to have a very bad day.

Here are ways you can ***Respond***: walk away from the bully as fast as you can, it may or may not be the best solution. The bully may follow you.

Run away from the bully as fast as you can, with your purpose being to find a responsible adult to help you.

However, unless you've been taught **"emergency running skills,"** this may not be a wise thing for you to do.

The bully could possibly chase and catch you.

If you have the confidence, you can try to talk your way out of the situation. If you choose this response, while talking, you must look the bully in the eyes.

If the bully is demanding you give him/her something of yours, you can choose to do so or not. **If the bully has a weapon, give him what he/she wants, you must quickly comply**.

If the bully has no weapon and he/she decides to get physical with you,

Your last response, because you have no other choice, is to get physical, too.

However, to fend off a bully physically, requires certain self-defense skills. Especially ones where no punches are thrown by you, but the bully is put under your mental or physical control.

You will need specific training to learn these skills so your reaction can be brave and bold.

Relax, React, Respond in a bully or emergency situation must be done by you just as fast as the lights went on and off when you were "hitting the light switch."

You will need specialized training and practice to Relax, React, and Respond in an uncomfortable situation, and to hopefully do so without a **glitch**.

Al Johnson

Never Argue With A Bully

Never Argue with a Bully

Bullies don't mind yelling and arguing. It's really what they commonly prefer to do.

There could be times when the bully wants to argue with you.

Never argue with a bully, if you do, you will be wasting precious energy that could be put to better use.

Never argue with a bully, by doing so, you'll be **stooping** to a low level of **existence** where bullies reside. Hanging around low-level places is not what a kid like you should ever do.

Never argue with a bully, cautiously walk away, leave the scene if necessary, and seek adult help.

By walking away from the bully, the bully is left to argue with no one but himself/herself.

Never argue with a bully, an argument can quickly result in a physical fight.

Please always remember, if a bully wants to start an argument with you, respond by quickly taking flight.

There could be a time when you are **tempted to argue** with a bully because you want to make a point or you don't like what a bully says.

However, the bottom line is, never argue with a bully under any circumstance. It's never worth it to do so, no matter what the bully says!

Al Johnson

The Same Kid

The Same Kid

Bullies will always pick on the same kid over and over if the bully has their way. That's just what bullies do.

Make sure the "same kid" the bully keeps picking on, is not you.

If a bully decides to hassle you and you don't want to be that "same kid," you must discourage him/her the very first time.

The bully must know immediately you're quite serious about not being bullied, not even one time.

Bullies do not like a strong and confident challenge by another kid in any way.

Bullies look for easy victims to be their **continuous prey**.

Put into practice what your parents, teachers, and other responsible adults have taught you about how best to handle the bully.

Then, you'll always be the "same kid" walking around with an air of magnificent self-confidence. Confidence in a kid is not what a bully wants to ever see.

Al Johnson

Using The Word Please

Using the Word Please

The word "please" is a polite word for kids to use.

Kids learn to use the word "please" from their loving parents even before they are old enough for school.

Do you think a bully uses the word "please" a lot, if ever at all?

Would a bully say to another kid, please give me your jacket, shoes, or money? I don't think so, that's not a bully's personality call!

So, it's **highly probable** a bully might be very uncomfortable with the word "please," no matter who it came from.

Well, if a bully wants to take advantage of you, here's how to hopefully penetrate his/her **fake protective shield**, possibly leaving the bully feeling a little dumb.

If an aggressive bully grabs you with a firm grip, and they just might, the grab makes the bully feel he/she has control and power over you.

No matter how afraid you are, you must look the bully in the eyes with a real confident and **magnetized look**, in fact, with a cold hard stare, even if it's hard for you to do.

In a polite, but firm voice, ask the bully to "please let you go, you're not looking for trouble." You may not use these exact words in this manner, but make sure you strongly say "please."

Politeness, a firm voice, and "please" will probably not **compute** very well in the bully's mind. However, it certainly should help set your mind at ease.

Repeat your please phrase more than once if the bully doesn't let you go, each time with the same politeness, but in a **firmer voice** and colder stare.

At this point, you have correctly decided that no matter what, you have to get away from there.

You have now created the unusual, the unexpected in the bully's mind, hopefully, putting the bully in a state of confusion. For a bully, handling confusion is always hard.

If the bully lets you go, and hopefully he/she does, simply **walk briskly away** with caution, always remaining on guard.

If the bully does not let you go, you must break away with force if you have to.

Shout your please phrase at the top of your lungs, looking the bully in the eye, as you break away. This may be necessary, and unfortunately, what you must do.

Be prepared to effectively defend yourself, if that's what it takes.

We hope the outcome will be that the **misguided and ill-mannered** bully, without any physical harm to you, him or her, will now allow you to peacefully walk away.

Al Johnson

Bully Stuck in the Mud

Bully Stuck in the Mud

Bullies like smooth sailing when they set out to bully someone.

Bullies expect to do what they want the way they want to do it. Bullies always feel strong and powerful, before, during, and after their bullying is done.

The chances are the bully will be successful if the kid picked out to be the victim allows a bully to continually have his/her way.

Because the overwhelming majority of kids are not trained in effective methods of handling the bully, far too many kids are bullied every day.

Bullies enjoy **disrupting** and confusing a kid's life any way they can.

Bullying will always continue with its ugliness if the bully knows he/she has the upper hand.

No matter how hard it is for you to do, you must tell the bully to leave you alone. Speak in an **empowering confident tone** as you've never spoken to the bully before.

Bullies don't like surprises, especially unexpected ones where you refuse to be bullied anymore.

This extremely confident and new you just may send a powerful message to the bully, with an **impacting thunderous thud**.

If you do this with strong conviction, you will leave the bully very uncomfortable, and just another misguided bully stuck in the mud.

Al Johnson

Do You Really Enjoy Being Mean?

Do You Really Enjoy Being Mean?

On the surface, you're almost always mean to other kids.

Do you really enjoy being mean? After you bully a kid, are you really happy about the bullying you did?

Does your meanness come from your heart or somewhere along the way was it conveniently placed in your mind?

Do you really enjoy being mean, finding it too hard to pleasantly smile much of the time?

Do you really enjoy being mean? That frown you continually wear, will bring early and permanent wrinkles to your face.

Do you really enjoy being mean? Have you ever thought about all the time it takes to be mean? That's precious time you put to waste.

The next time you take a shower and you're standing in front of your mirror, feeling all refreshed and clean,

If you're a bully, ask the kid looking back at you, and be truly honest with yourself: "Do you really enjoy being mean?"

Al Johnson

Bullying Must Not Be Taken Lightly

Bullying Must Not Be Taken Lightly

Often when a kid tells an adult about a bullying problem they're having, it's brushed aside as kids just growing up.

Any form of bullying must not be taken lightly; harsh words can quickly turn into a push or shove.

A push or shove can quickly lead to a fight.

These unwanted occurrences can possibly be prevented, if the adult has the necessary foresight.

Bullying must not be taken lightly. Bullied kids could be scarred for life.

The pain and fear a bullied kid suffers emotionally can cut like a knife.

When teachers, parents, and other responsible adults witness minor interactions between kids, which seem a bit out of the norm,

They should immediately **intercede**. If it turns out to be innocent play, it's better to be wrong than to allow a kid to possibly be bullied and harmed.

Adults, and kids, too, must be alert and aware of occurring events at school, in the neighborhood, and on the internet. We all must take notice carefully.

Because any form of bullying, must not be taken lightly.

Al Johnson

Suspending The Wrong Kid

Suspending the Wrong Kid

Are we not suspending the wrong kid from school when we suspend the kid who has been bullied along with the bully, too?

In this case, the bullied kid is suspended when he/she, because of no adult help, and as a last resort, fights back. Unfortunately, the bully gave the kid little choice. What's a bullied kid in this harmful situation left to do?

Since there is no adult around to help a kid, an aggressive grab or blow can happen in a split second, and usually does.

Are we rightfully saying to a kid who is backed into a corner, he/she has no right to self-defend without being suspended, no matter what the bully physically does?

Do we want kids fighting at school? No, we emphatically don't!

Do we want kids being physically bullied at school, especially when there's no adult around? No, we emphatically don't!

We must give kids being bullied all the knowledge and skills we can for them to effectively avoid, eliminate, and prevent the bullying.

Suspending the bullied kid for protecting himself/herself when there was no adult around, does little, if anything, to effectively and permanently stop the bullying.

By suspending the wrong kid, we give the bully more power. The likelihood of him/her bullying the same kid again, will be quite high.

A bully usually ceases to bully a kid when that kid aggressively fights back, hopefully, with unique mental toughness only.
Bullies do not do well with the unexpected and element of surprise.

If we do all we can to empower kids to effectively solve their bullying problem with limited adult or peer intervention,

The question of "are we suspending the wrong kid," will likely never have to be addressed with school administrative-punishment-attention.

Al Johnson

Confuse The Bully

Confuse the Bully

Confuse the bully in any way you can, if a bully gets in your face.

Confusion is a **tremendous** weapon for a kid to use against a bully. It will always make a bully feel off balance and out of place.

Bullies expect everything to go their way, that's why they keep bullying. In the bully's world, that's the way it's always been.

Confusion changes everything. If a kid knows ways to confuse the bully, what a powerful message confusion will send.

Confuse the bully with unusual and unique words and phrases, but never use profanity. Use actions and anything unexpected, totally out of the norm.

By you successfully confusing the bully, you have a much better chance of eliminating or preventing any of the bully's intended mental or physical harm.

Role-playing confusing techniques against a bully are necessary skills for kids to know and learn to use.

A great **permanent possession** for kids targeted for bullying to have, is an **arsenal of self-confidence** and necessary skills to quickly make a bully become **disjointed** and confused.

All kids must absolutely believe,

It's in their best interest to know multiple ways to confuse the bully, if ever necessary, and can confidently do so, with the greatest of ease.

Al Johnson

I'm Stronger Than You

I'm Stronger than You

I'm stronger than you.

You may find that hard to believe since you're six feet tall, and I'm only five feet two.

True strength has very little to do with physical size.

A kid's or anyone else's real strength is determined by what they choose to do with their heart and mind.

You've chosen to bully kids. Unfortunately, that choice has made you extremely weak.

Because of **misguided intelligence**, your weakness is obviously far too difficult for you to see.

Yes, I'm stronger than you because I treat all kids and people deserving, with **dignity and respect**.

I have awesome power because, I would never even think about bullying another kid. Therefore, when it comes to disrespecting other kids, there's nothing for me to regret.

Every day you bully another kid, unfortunately, without you realizing it, you become weaker and weaker in your heart and mind.

Your weakness will surely eat away at you in unpleasant ways, if you continue bullying over your lifetime.

You'll be an unhappy bully, even as an adult, with very few, if any true friends.

Being a bully shouldn't be the message you continue to want to send.

You can easily have **wonderful inner strength**, as all good kids do.

Just stop your bullying, stop now! Until you make the worthwhile decision to quit, kids like me will always be so much stronger than you.

Al Johnson

Social Skills Too

Social Skills Too

Kids primarily learn academic skills in school.

However, we must teach kids social skills, too.

Kids learn lots of social skills from caring and loving parents as they grow.

They need to build on social skills taught in the home. **There are real world social skills, too, kids must know**.

When anyone decides to bully others, it is obvious they lack social skills.

Even if kids aren't bullies, but use profanity and foul language a lot, as so many do, they are lacking social skills.

If kids are disrespectful to parents, teachers, and other adults, they lack social skills.

It's apparent a kid would not become a bully if he/she had proper social skills.

Learning math, English, reading, writing, and science are all important vital subjects kids must learn and do.

However, it is just as important and vital for them to be taught, and they effectively acquire and retain, proper social skills, too.

Al Johnson

Bullies Are Without Self-Confidence

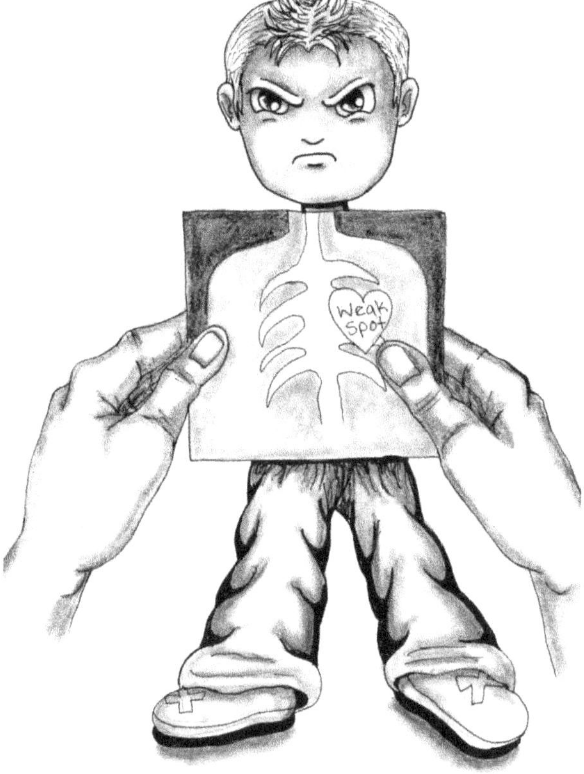

Bullies Are without Self-Confidence

Did you know that bullies are without self-confidence? However, that's a message bullies try hard not to send.

Sure, on the surface bullies act tough and strong. However, self-confidence doesn't come from surface appearance, but from within.

Bullies hide their doubt and lack of self-confidence by seeking out those who lack more self-confidence than they do.

Once a bully finds a kid without self-confidence, he/she will dominate over and over again, sticking to him/her like very hard to remove glue.

If kids know bullies are without self-confidence, kids will have the upper hand.

Kids will have a much better chance of not being bullied because of what they clearly understand.

If a bully comes around you and gets in your face,

With your imaginary X-ray vision, you can look right through the bully, quickly locating the bully's apparent non-confident place.

You can tell the bully in a calm, but firm voice, "You will not bully me!"

"Because I know your secret. It's crystal clear as can be!"

You should tell the bully, "I'm going to leave you in dreaded isolation, precariously straddling your self-made-sharply pointed-picket fence."

Goodbye! Have a nice life! "You're a bully. I'm not afraid of you! Bullies are always without real self-confidence!"

Al Johnson

Have You Ever Thought About Being A Bully?

Have You Ever Thought about Being a Bully?

Have you ever thought about being a bully, although you haven't quite made up your mind?

This poem is to help you come to the correct conclusion by the time you hear or read the last line.

What would make you want to be a bully, anyway? Where did such a **misplaced and twisted idea** come from?

The **mere** thought of wanting to become a bully is nothing but dumb.

Do you really respect a bully that is feared by kids because of being falsely powerful and strong?

The fear a bully instills in other kids and the strength and power the bully may have will eventually be taken away. It will not last very long.

Have you ever thought about being a bully? Do you think bullies are really appreciated and looked up to?

Bullies do not deserve true appreciation or respect because they seek to control and **belittle** good kids like me and you.

Have you ever thought about being a bully? Do you know that a bully could be in the presence of many kids, yet be on an island, alone, all by himself/herself?

Do you really want to feel isolated, alone, and unaware that if you're a bully, you're in **dire need** of immediate help?

Have you ever thought about being a bully? Bullies aren't fun to be around.

Even if a bully is joking and laughing on the outside, on the inside the bully's heart is wearing an ugly stain and frown.

Have you ever thought about being a bully? If so, immediately and permanently erase it from your mind.

Any kid that becomes a bully could reach the point of no return, and never be looked up to for being respectful, friendly, and kind.

Al Johnson

I Feel Sorry For Bullies

I Feel Sorry for Bullies

I feel sorry for bullies. I don't know why they act the way they do.

When it comes to all the fun, nice, and worthwhile stuff a kid can do in life, bullies don't seem to have a clue.

I feel sorry for bullies. They seem to be unhappy all the time.

I feel sorry for bullies. They all have twisted minds.

I feel sorry for bullies. They have no **compassion** and don't tell the truth.

I feel sorry for bullies. They usually don't do very well in school.

I feel sorry for bullies. They really don't feel good about themselves, unless they make another kid feel bad.

I feel sorry for bullies. Their lives to me, seem so sad.

You might be thinking, why a kid like me should feel sorry for bullies, because of the stupid stuff they do.

I feel sorry for bullies because if they don't stop bullying, they will never experience all the real cool, fun, and healthy stuff that kids like me are into.

Al Johnson

Social Network Caution

Social Network Caution

Social networks on the internet are popular with kids, especially teens.

Parents should put a block on anything their kids could encounter on line that should not be heard or seen.

Kids you may not like the block, but it's being done because your parents want to protect you.

If you find a way around the block, getting access to social networks, be responsible; avoid doing anything on line your parents have instructed you not to do.

You'll be showing respect for your parents, yourself, and tremendous restraint, strength, and wisdom because you may have been tempted to.

Teens especially, if you're allowed to use social networks, heed your parents' instructions. **There are always people on line looking to take negative advantage of a teen like you**.

Do not hold conversations in "chat rooms" with anyone you **initially meet** on line. To do so is one of the most dangerous things you can do.

If anyone on line offers to meet you in person, without any thought or hesitation; telling your parents immediately is what you must do!

Many kids have been taken advantage of by people they've met on line.

Always use social network caution skills when you are on line. If you do so, you will be a kid or teen that will successfully make it through your youthful years safe from harm, and more than likely, just fine.

Al Johnson

The Light At The End Of The Tunnel

The Light at the End of the Tunnel

Although the **dark and dingy tunnel** you live in stretches for miles because of the bullying you do,

There is a light at the end of the tunnel out there waiting for you.

You are unable to see the light now. Your bullying ways keep you spinning your wheels in the dark.

If you continue to bully kids, reaching the light at the end of the tunnel will become extremely hard.

If you change course, stop your bullying, very quickly, you'll see a **glimmer** of light not so far away.

As you continue along your non-bullying path, the light at the end of the tunnel will grow brighter and brighter each day.

There will be lots of fun new friends and **proud accomplishments** at the end of the tunnel that will come into your life.

You will joke, laugh, and smile like never before. You will have rid yourself of the **strife**.

Up until now, you probably never thought about the light at the end of the tunnel that's been so difficult for you to see.

You should not only think about it, but seek to have it **encircle** you for a lifetime. Amid the light at the end of the tunnel, is a wonderful and very cool place for a kid to be.

Al Johnson

The Stranger On The Internet

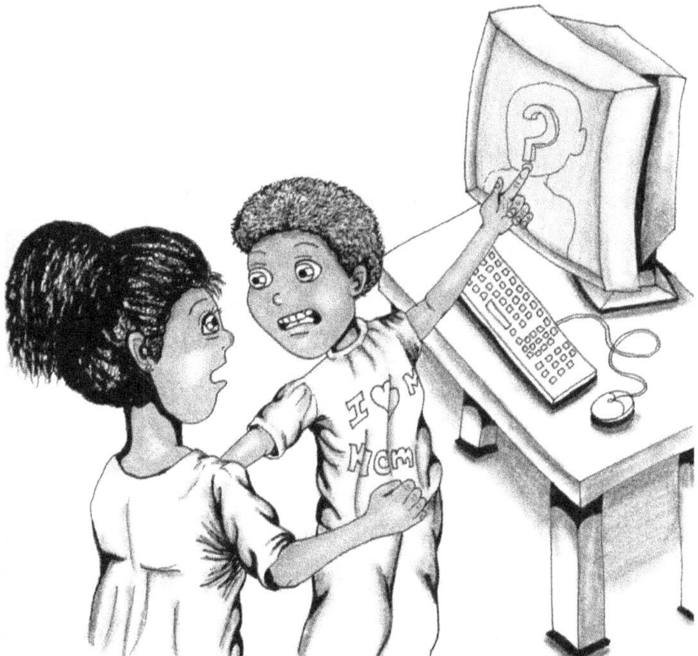

The Stranger on the Internet

The stranger on the internet should be treated just as a stranger on the street.

Parents and responsible adults have told kids never talk to strangers they might meet.

The stranger on the internet is constantly on the **prowl**, looking for any kid they can **influence and convince**.

The stranger on the internet knows confusing, slick, and **enticing** ways causing a kid to let down his/her defense.

Kids, if you ever come across a stranger on the internet,

Do not, under any circumstance, chat with them. Conversations with strangers on the internet can only lead to **regret**.

Quickly tell your parents or any responsible adult about the stranger on the internet.

Hopefully, you can do this while the stranger is still online.

Then, if the stranger is a bad person that commits crimes against kids, maybe the police can catch him/her quickly. They'll then be the stranger on the internet hopefully, for the very last time.

Al Johnson

Listen To How I Talk Now

Listen to How I Talk Now!

The first time I was bullied, I didn't like it very much, but I wasn't left feeling **devastated** and down in the dumps.

I thought the first time was going to be the last. Man, was I wrong. There was much more bullying that would come.

The more I was bullied, the worse I felt. My whole **demeanor** quickly became very meek and weak.

Going around in such a sad state is not how a kid should have to be.

When the bully came around me, I would look at the ground every single time.

I couldn't look the bully in the eyes. The bully was in control, which made me feel lousy, while the bully felt just fine.

Before a bully came into my life, I always talked with in a strong voice, with confidence. **The more I was bullied, the more my voice grew soft and faint.**

My self-confidence was **shattered**. Stuff I used to do that came easy, was now too hard, especially school work. The first thing out of my mouth now was, "I can't."

My parents, teachers, and other adults had a long talk with me.

One kid who was once bullied, told me how he/she defeated the bully.

Lots of kids told me that I must stand up to the bully, using all the inner strengths I probably never knew I had.

They all told me that no way could I allow a bully to make me feel weak and sad.

I quickly realized how weak my voice had become whenever the bully was in my face.

My voice has always been a great **asset** of mine. People would always tell me I had a strong voice that could make a building shake.

So, I practiced getting my strong voice and confidence back for a while at home.

The words that I practiced to say to the bully were, "You will not bully me ever again! It is in your best interest, to leave me alone!"

"Practice makes perfect," my parents always say. You know what, they are right.

My **thunderous voice** and confidence is back, those meek and weak days have forever taken flight.

What a great feeling I have now and will forever more! Wow!

These words are just for you, **insignificant, meek** and weak bully:

"Listen to how I talk now!"

Al Johnson

Suggest You Don't Challenge Me

I Suggest You Don't Challenge Me

If you are a bully thinking about giving me a bad time, I suggest you don't challenge me.

I'm not looking for trouble, an argument or a fight; however, I will not be the victim you want me to be.

Bullies enjoy challenging kids with the **intent** of mentally or physically **overpowering** them, and making them feel afraid.

I'm not afraid of you. I suggest you don't challenge me, hope you're listening carefully to what I say.

It's in your best interest to not challenge me.

In fact, it's in your best interest to immediately stop being a bully.

Bullying another kid is one of the worst things any kid can do.

You have a good heart and mind like most kids, why not let the goodness in you shine through.

However, just in case you **inappropriately** continue to seek kids to challenge and bully,

May I kindly remind you once again, and for the very last time, don't look in my direction for a victim. I strongly suggest you don't challenge me.

Al Johnson

What Is Going On Inside Your Head?

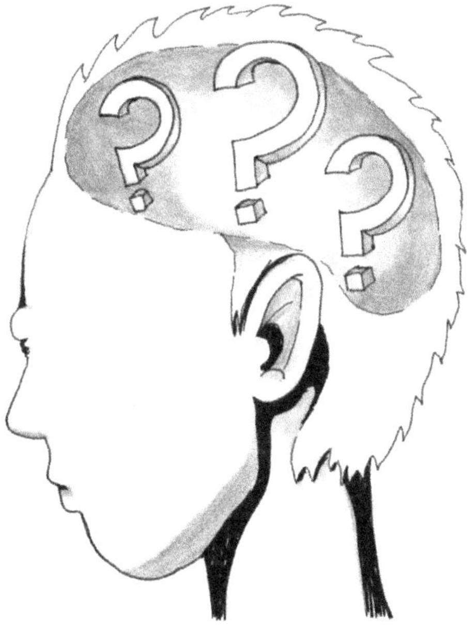

What Is Going on inside Your Head?

You seem to enjoy being a bully, always acting all tough and stuff.

You pick on kids, call them names, and take things from them. When it comes to bullying kids, you seem to never get enough.

What is going on inside your head to make you do the stupid bullying stuff you do?

Are your intelligent brain cells twisted, misplaced, or maybe missing altogether? What's wrong with you?

Definitely, something wrong is going on inside your head, or you would not do the nasty and ugly things you do.

When it comes to treating all kids and people with respect, you refuse, or you don't seem to have a clue.

What's going on inside your head? There appears to be nothing but darkness up there. Before it's too late, you need to turn on the light.

You need to see the world from a different point of view, **abolishing** the wrong forever and **embracing** what's right.

Please, immediately stop bullying other kids. Take **heed** to what I've said.

If you do, you will never again have to hear anyone say in a negative way, "What's going on inside your head?"

Al Johnson

A Bully's Negative Impact

A Bully's Negative Impact

Bullies don't consider the **negative impact** their bullying can cause.

The bully setting out to create a negative impact doesn't care because his/her attitude and **persona** have **flaws**.

A bully's negative impact could mean a bullied kid could have trouble sleeping at night.

A bully's negative impact could mean a once happy kid could grow sad, go into an unhealthy shell, and just not mentally or physically feel right.

A bully's negative impact could mean a bullied kid is afraid to go to school. Good grades once made, turn into bad.

A bully's negative impact could cause the loss of one's self-esteem and the self-confidence they once had.

A bully's negative impact could cause a bullied kid to be lonely and confused in a **disheartening** way.

For any bully who may be hearing or reading this, can you somehow see the negative impact your bullying has on others on any given day?

In case you do not understand the seriousness of your bullying, allow me to give you one final heartbreaking fact.

Every sad thing that could happen to a kid being bullied, could grow like a untreated cancer cell inside the body. It can destroy a kid's will to carry on, all because of a bully's negative impact.

Al Johnson

Never Physically Fight-Unless

Never Physically Fight–Unless

Because adults are almost never around when a kid is being bullied, there are certain choices a kid has to immediately make.

If bullying becomes physical, what methods to insure his/her safety does a kid have the right to take?

Societal laws clearly state we all have the right to **reasonably defend** ourselves or our families against unlawful physical harm.

Bullying is unlawful. With no adult around preventing a bully's assault, kids have the right to defend themselves against a bully's possible physical harm.

I'm not **advocating** physical fighting for kids being bullied, not at all!

Physical confrontation can be brutal and ugly, and should always be for a kid or adult, the very last call.

However, today, because the focus for so many, including kids, is **self-gratification** and **inappropriately wearing the mantel** of 'it's all about me,'

Kids must send a strong and powerful message to the bully in any lawful way, to **insure** the bully fails to succeed.

Kids should get proper self-defense training, just in case, for their safety. This could be a **necessity** for kids to do.

I'm emphatically stating to all kids facing a bullying problem, never, ever physically fight the bully unless you're properly trained. It's always your last resort, even when no one else is there to help protect you.

Al Johnson

Make This Day The Last

Make This Day the Last

Make this day the last that you choose to bully another kid.

If you have bullied another kid, there is no way you can be proud of what you did.

Make this day the last when, for no good reason, other than self-satisfaction, you call kids inappropriate names.

For this, you should be **apologetic** and very ashamed.

Make this day the last you spread rumors on line about a kid. When in your heart, you know what you're saying is wrong and untrue.

Have you ever thought about how you would feel if the same kind of **vicious rumors** were being spread all over the internet about you?

Make this day the last you go around all day looking mean and acting tough.

Try wearing a smile, have a **hearty laugh,** say to yourself, and really mean it, when it comes to bullying another kid, I've had enough.

Life is about making positive changes as we live and grow.

When it comes to you being a bully, make this day the last. If you do, your life will be full of so much more fun and good cheer, much more than you ever know.

Al Johnson

Now I Can Laugh, Joke, And Have Fun Again

Now I Can Laugh, Joke, and Have Fun Again

Because of being bullied, for a while I stopped laughing and having fun with my friends.

I didn't feel very good about myself. My self-confidence had **worn** thin.

It was hard for me to look the bully in the eyes.

I began feeling sadder and sadder as each day passed by.

I'd wake up at night thinking about my bully problem. It wasn't easy for me to get back to sleep.

I was at a loss; I didn't know what to do or who to talk to. I was in **desperate** need.

My parents and teachers saw the unhealthy change in me, so they pulled me aside.

At first, I did not want to tell them about being bullied, but they convinced me that bullying is serious and not something to hide.

The more we talked, the better I felt. They told me things to do that made me feel stronger. I quickly began to believe my bullying problem would soon end.

Guess what! Now I can laugh, joke, and have fun again.

Al Johnson

Eye To Eye

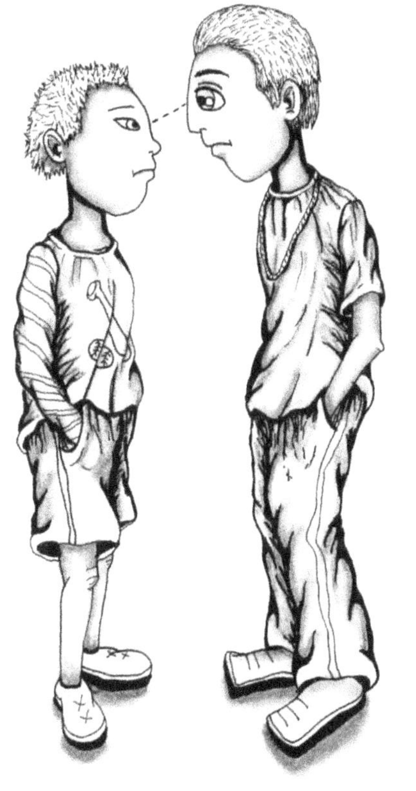

Eye to Eye

It's not easy looking someone straight in the eyes, especially if it's a bully.

The bully might think my dog-stare is a challenge and want to pick a fight with me.

Adults have told me that to go eye to eye with someone shows a tremendous amount of self-confidence.

Self-confidence is what bullies want to destroy in a kid, that's **a bully's primary intent**.

I always look down or away when the bully gets in my face, and the bully sees the **discomfort** and fear written all over me.

So, I'm bullied more and more, giving all the power to the bully.

The very next time, I'm going eye to eye with the bully. I wonder when I do, will there be a change in his/her attitude?

It may be hard at first to go eye to eye with the bully, but it's something I must do.

Here's a great thought; the bully may just **crumble** a bit under my visual pressure, becoming weaker and weaker as the seconds go by.

I now think I have the pride, confidence, and high self-esteem to effectively handle the bully, eye to eye.

Al Johnson

How Many Times?

How Many Times?

How many times have you bullied another kid?

How many times have you felt sorry for what you did?

How many times have you called kids names you knew would hurt?

Have you ever asked yourself what all the unnecessary name-calling is really worth?

How many times have you pushed or shoved kids because you were bigger and stronger than them?

Do you get pleasure from mentally or physically harming other kids? If so, **from where does your twisted way of thinking stem?**

How many times have you made another kid cry because of something you said or did?

How many times will you continue to bully kids?

You probably can't count the times because it's been so many.

Hello! For your information, when it comes to bullying another kid, one time is more than a plenty.

Why don't you immediately stop bullying other kids? There's an ideal place for you to join the nice-and-kind-kid's-line.

Then, zero will be your answer, when it comes to being a bully, the next time you're asked, how many times?

Al Johnson

I Once Bullied Too

I Once Bullied Too

Because of how I am now, you might find it hard to believe I once bullied, too.

I used to hassle kids, call them names, push and shove them. Yes, I did the stupid stuff bullies do.

At that time, I thought being a bully was really cool.

Yep, I once I bullied, too.

I never thought much about what I was doing. I only thought about myself.

Then, one day I saw another kid being bullied by someone else.

I saw the bully laugh and the kid cry.

The bullied kid looked so sad. I almost had tears in my eyes.

At that moment, it became clear to me bullying was wrong. No one has the right to make a kid feel bad that way.

I stood up for that kid. I never bullied again, after what I saw that day.

So, if you are a bully, I ask you to please immediately stop! You can find many more positive things in your life to do.

Take it from me you can stop your bullying. I should know. I once bullied, too!

Al Johnson

There's Always Someone Tougher Than You

There's Always Someone Tougher than You

You obviously think you are the toughest kid at school.

You might be tough, but there's always someone tougher than you.

You enjoy being tough and having lots of kids scared of you.

However, you're going to find out one day the hard way, there's always someone tougher than you.

You'll meet your match and be **devastated** by the outcome.

You'll try to bully and challenge the wrong kid, and quickly realize, oops, that move was dumb.

The confident kid that will be tougher than you, will not back down from you at all.

You will melt like butter when the kid stands up to you, all confident, strong, and tall.

Oh, for your clarification, you should know, this kid will stand tall, yet in physical inches, may be half your size.

He/She will look up at you, then look you straight in the eyes.

You always could dominate kids smaller than you. It's always been so easy for you to do.

This small kid will not be afraid. You'll know by the look in his/her eyes. Avoid being totally embarrassed in the future, stop your stupid bullying now! There's always someone tougher than you.

Al Johnson

Take A Long Look In Your Mirror

Take a Long Look in Your Mirror

Hey kids! I invite you to take a long look in your mirror. Do you like what you see?

You shouldn't like what you see at all, if you see a bully.

Try a different angle; turn sideways for a profile. Now do you like what you see?

You shouldn't like what you see at all, if you see a bully.

Okay, how about you turn your back to the mirror and look over your shoulder behind you. Now do you like what you see?

You shouldn't like what you see at all, if you see a bully.

Turn back around facing the mirror again, take another long look. This time force yourself to bring a broad smile to your face.

Yes, your smile will be forced and fake because bullies don't wear natural bright smiles that remain in place.

Okay, let's try this, while you're still facing your mirror, say out loud, "I'm proud to be a disrespectful bully, it's one of the coolest things a kid could do."

Your mirror is now just like a lie detector, by the look on your face, and the tone of your voice, you and your mirror know what you just said wasn't really the truth.

So, what is the lesson to be learned from the long look in your mirror, you might be saying? Was there a worthwhile lesson that is important to be made?

Yes! If you immediately stop bullying forever, the very next time you look in your mirror from every angle, you'll see a truly warm, smiling, and kind hearted face.

Al Johnson

Awareness

Awareness

A kid's best chance of not being bullied is to be keenly aware of bullies long before it's too late.

Kids must know **subtle signs** a bully might **reveal** and what those signs could **indicate**.

Too often today, a kid's attention is constantly focused on I-pads, cell phones, and any other electronic device.

Kids are not nearly as focused on their environment, people in it, or potential trouble that could be **lurking** in plain sight.

Bullies bank on kids being unaware. This makes it easy for a kid to be caught off guard.

Being caught off guard, surprised, and confused makes a kid's chances of avoiding and defeating the bully very hard.

The only good thing about bullies is that they're easily recognized, if a kid knows what to look for. Bullies and potential ones tend to have **similar traits**.

They call kids names, push, and shove, they want things their way. They seldom smile and, when patience is needed, the bully has none. **Bullies are ill equipped to patiently wait**.

There are other unpleasant signs a bully has; the ones mentioned are just an important few.

Kids, please learn to recognize them, you'll be more aware and have a much better chance of avoiding the bully if you do.

You need to stay alert, aware, and stay away from the bully. It is what you must learn how to effectively do.

By sharpening your awareness skills, the outcome will be bad for the bully and very good for you.

Al Johnson

Bullies Be Gone Song

Bullies Be Gone Song

By Al Johnson

Verse 1

It ain't okay to call me names
It ain't okay for you to defame
Just because I'm not like you
You got no right to abuse
Did someone in your past bully you?

Chorus

Bullies be gone forever—from this day on
You got no right to bully me, bullies be gone
Is your mind so (that) weak? Could you be jealous of me?
Just leave with your nasty tone, bullies be gone!

(Repeat last line 3 times)

Verse 2

Don't know what happen in your past
There must be pain that still last
Try smiling more it just may work,
To rid you of a scar that hurts
Did someone in your past bully you?

Back to Chorus

Bridge

Get outta my life, go away
I won't be a (your) victim another day
I'll stand tall, look you in the eye
Your best choice is to pass me by
Did someone in your past bully you?

Back to Chorus—Out

Bullies Be Gone—Rap Version

By Al Johnson & Kenny Terry

Adlib & Intro

Hey, let's get real with this bullying thing.
Look in the mirror, what reflection does it bring?
If you're a bully or you wanna be,
Gotta change your attitude real fast, just like one, two, three

(Background hook line)

Verse 1

It ain't okay for you to call me names.
It ain't okay for you to defame.
Just because I'm not like you,
You ain't got no right to abuse.
Did someone in your past bully you?
Bully be gone,
Forever, from this day on
You ain't got no right, no right to bully me
Is your mind so weak, could you be jealous of me?

Hook

Hey, hey, bullies be gone

(adlib line—No more bullying!)

Go away, go away, bullies be gone

(adlib line—If get bullied, don't keep it a secret!)

Verse 2

Don't know what happen in your past
There must be pain still that last.
Try smiling more it just may work
To rid you of a scar that still hurts.
Did someone in your past bully you?

Bullies got no confidence, none at all

So you bully kids you think are weak,

To make you feel strong and tall,

You gone fall! You gone fall!

Back to Hook

You bully a kid just one time, it's one time too much

The kid you bully could suffer over and over again, and with reality lose touch

If you're a bully or wanna be

Gotta change your attitude real fast, just like one, two, three

Hook—Adlib—Out

Somewhere inside you, a nice kid's waiting to shine.

Let that kid out, let'm out, right now is the perfect time.

www.ingramcontent.com/pod-product-compliance
Lightning Source LLC
Chambersburg PA
CBHW081349080526
44588CB00016B/2421
* 9 7 8 1 9 3 8 0 1 5 6 9 4 *